YOU'RE ALREADY HOME

Kabîr's Vision
of the Spiritual Realm

Copyright © 2023, Anamchara Books.

All rights reserved. No part of this publication may be reproduced or transmitted for commercial purposes, except for brief quotations, without written permission of the publisher. Churches and other noncommercial interests may reproduce portions of this book without the express written permission of Anamchara Books, provided that the text does not exceed 500 words or 5 percent of the entire book, whichever is less, and that the text is not material quoted from another publisher. When reproducing text from this book, include the following credit line: "From *You're Already Home: Kabir's Vision of the Spiritual Realm*, published by Anamchara Books. Used by permission."

Anamchara Books
Vestal, New York 13850
www.AnamcharaBooks.com

Paperback ISBN: 978-1-62524-858-9
eBook ISBN: 978-1-62524-859-6

Cover design by Ellyn Sanna.

YOU'RE ALREADY HOME

Kabîr's Vision of the Spiritual Realm

put into modern language by

ELLYN SANNA

Introduction

Kabîr's deep spirituality could not be contained by religion. Born to Muslim parents in India in the middle of the fifteenth century, as a young adult he became a Hindu. Ultimately, however, his religion was simply love.

Historians know only a little about the details of Kabîr's life. He was a skilled musician, as well as a poet, who supported his wife and children as a weaver of fabric. His poetry reveals his love of ordinary life; in the relationships and responsibilities of home, he found all the challenge he needed for the renunciation of the ego and the encounter with Absolute Love. He believed the Song of Love "spreads everywhere, infinitely," and he condemned the hypocrisy and elitism of institutionalized religion.

The passionate poetry of the Sufi mystics (Rumi, Hafiz, and others) inspired Kabîr, and he dreamed of uniting this intimate understanding of the Divine as

Beloved with the theology of more traditional Hinduism. During his lifetime, Hindu-Muslim strife raged, and the polarization was deep and entrenched. And yet, as Evelyn Underhill noted in her introduction to Rabindranath Tagore's translation of Kabîr's poetry, in Kabîr's spiritual thinking, "apparently antagonistic streams of intense spiritual culture met . . . and it is one of the outstanding characteristics of Kabîr's genius that he was able in his poems to fuse them into one." Kabîr was a master of spiritual synthesis. As evidence of that, today, both Muslims and Hindus claim him as their saint.

Kabîr, however, had little use for doctrine or theology—"The Beloved," he wrote, "can never be found in abstractions and generalizations"—and he was contemptuous of religious trappings, including the rituals and the physical self-denial practiced by many ascetics of his day. Union with God, Kabîr taught, is the goal of all human beings, and it is open to anyone and everyone who simply follows the path of love. As Underhill noted, "The whole apparatus of piety, Hindu and Moslem alike—the temple and mosque, [statue] and holy water, scriptures and priests—were denounced by this inconveniently clear-sighted poet as mere substitutes for reality; dead things intervening between the soul and its love."

Underhill also said of Kabîr that he was a "hater of religious exclusivism," who sought to open the door for us all to enter "into the liberty of the children of God." His relationship with the Divine transcended all religious categories or doctrinal definitions. Instead, he was a faithful lover of "that Supreme Spirit Whom he knew and adored, and to Whose joyous friendship he sought to induct the souls" of all people.

Kabîr's unorthodox beliefs made both Muslims and Hindus consider him a heretic. Although both religions claimed him as their own after his death, during his lifetime, he faced persecution, fear, and hatred. When he was nearly sixty years old, he was banished from his hometown of Benares and spent the rest of his life in exile.

The day of Kabîr's death, like the date of his birth, is unclear. According to some accounts, he died at the age of eighty; other traditions claim he lived until he was well past one hundred. In all likelihood, he died at some point in the early decades of the sixteenth century.

When he died, legend tells that both his Muslim and Hindu disciples wanted to claim possession of his body; the Muslims wanted to bury it, and the Hindus wanted to burn it. As they argued over the corpse, Kabîr appeared and said, "Lift my shroud and look at what lies within." When they did so, they found the body had disappeared; in its place was a heap of flowers. The implication is that Kabîr's life left behind a fragrance that could not be confined to a single religion.

At the time of Kabîr's death, his poems did not exist in written form (in fact, he probably could not read and write at all). Instead, he memorized his poetry and taught it to his disciples, who in turn passed it on orally for the next two centuries. Not until the seventeenth century were the poems compiled and written down

Because of this, many scholars question the authenticity of Kabîr's poetry as it is published today. As the words were passed along from generation to generation, they would have inevitably changed. His followers may have composed new poems, which were attributed to him. According to the tradition of the ancient world, this was not seen as dishonesty but as a way of honoring a teacher's wisdom.

Early in the twentieth century, Rabindranath Tagore, the Indian writer, composer, philosopher, social reformer, and painter, translated Kabîr's work into English. This book's modern-language interpretations of Kabîr's poems are based on Tagore's translation. Some scholars have accused Tagore of imprinting his own ideas onto Kabîr's—but another school of thought claim's that Tagore's personal theology was actually Kabîr's, rather than an original synthesis of Tagore's own.

Kabîr would probably not care either way. After all, he wrote, "Where is the difference between the ocean and its waves? The ocean and its waves are one body. When the wave rises, it is the water, and when it falls, it is the same water again. Can you see any difference? Because we name the wave, can it no longer be thought of as water?" It matters not if Tagore was the wave and Kabîr the ocean—or the other way around—for all water gives life, no matter its source or form.

Kabîr's love relationship with the Divine offers us today a resolution to the dualism so present in our modern thinking, which perceives a wall between the spiritual and physical worlds, as well as between humanity and the

Divine, between life and death, and between darkness and light. "There are in his universe no fences between the 'natural' and 'supernatural' worlds," wrote Underhill; "everything is a part of the creative Play of God, and therefore—even in its humblest details . . . the whole of creation is the Play of the Eternal Lover, the living, changing, growing expression" of Divine love and joy.

Kabîr believed that in the union of love we each find our true identity—the specific God-given identity that is unique to each of us. In unity, we do not lose our individuality, merging into a single, indistinguishable substance, but rather, in the reciprocal oneness of a love relationship, we find our most truly distinct selves.

> *God is in me, and God is in you,*
> *just as Life is in every seed. . . .*
> *Shed your ego, the false self,*
> *and seek God within you.*

Because we carry the Divine within our own beings, we no longer have to strive or seek; Divine rest and fulfillment are ours for the taking. We are already home.

Note on pronouns: Kabîr (and Tagore's translation of Kabîr) shifted the speaker's perspective back and forth from masculine to feminine, and also referred to the Beloved as both male and female. We have kept this approach, in the belief that gender is a Divine expression and that a fluid understanding of gender leaves room for "our Lover who swings and plays," who cannot, as Kabîr wrote, be contained by our ideas but is "always something different" from what we think or imagine.

NOW

Where are you looking for Me?
Look! I'm right here! I'm right beside you!
But you will not find Me in churches or mosques;
I am not in cathedrals or on holy mountains,
nor am I in rites and ceremonies,
prayers and self-denial.
If you really want to seek Me,
the only place you will find me is—
NOW
in this moment, in this breath,
for I am the Breath that breathes through all breath.
Cease your restless searching.
You are already home.

YOU ARE LIKE A FISH

You are like a fish that thinks it is dying of thirst
while all the while it is swimming in fresh water.
The Infinite One lives in you and with you,
in the four walls of your very own home,
and yet you search everywhere
for the meaning of life.

THE TRUE REALITY

The moon glows within my body,
the sun shines through my flesh,
but my blind eyes cannot see them.
The unstruck drum of Eternity booms within me;
but my deaf ears cannot hear it.
So long as we clamor for the *I* and the *Mine*,
our works accomplish nothing.
When all love of the *I* and the *Mine* is dead,
then the Divine work is done.
The purpose of work is to build the True Reality.
When that comes, then work is put away.
The flower blooms for the fruit:
when the fruit comes, the flower withers.

THE INFINITE

When God reveals God-Self,
the Divine is manifested,
and yet it is that which can never be seen.
As the seed is in the plant,
as the shade is in the tree,
as the void is in the sky,
as infinite forms are in the void—
so from beyond the Infinite,
the Infinite comes;
and from the Infinite the finite extends.

MANIFOLD AND INFINITE

The creature is in the Creator,
and the Creator is in the creature:
they are ever distinct, yet ever united.
The Creator is the tree, the seed, and the embryo.
The Creator is the flower, the fruit, and the shade.
The Creator is the sun, the light, and the lighted.
The Creator is both God and creature
and the illusion our eyes perceive.
The Creator is manifold in form, infinite in space;
God is the breath, the word, and the meaning.

EVERYWHERE

God is the limit and the limitless,
and beyond both the limited and the limitless
is God, the Pure Being.
God is the Immanent Mind
in both the Creator and in the creature.
The Supreme Soul manifests within the soul,
the Point manifests within the Supreme Soul,
and within the Point, the reflection is seen again.

WITHIN ME

Within my body are groves and glades,
and within my body is the Creator.
The seven oceans and the unnumbered stars
are all within me.
Both the gem and the jewel-appraiser
are there as well.
The Eternal sounds within me,
and the spring wells up forever.
Listen to me, my friend!
My Beloved is within me.

NO WORDS

O, how can I ever express
the secret words that describe my Beloved?
How can I say,
God is not like this,
and God is like that?
If I say God is within me,
I lessen the universe.
If I say God is only outside me, I lie.
God makes the inner and the outer worlds
as one, indivisible.
The conscious and the unconscious,
both are God's footstools.
God is neither manifest nor hidden;
neither revealed nor unrevealed.
There are no words to describe my Beloved.

A SINGLE WORD

You have drawn my love to you, Holy One.
I was asleep in my bedroom,
and Your voice woke me.
I was drowning in the deeps of the world's ocean,
and You saved me,
holding me in Your arms, O Holy One.
Only a single word—and you freed me
from all that bound me.
You have united my heart with Yours.

BE NAKED

I have been playing with my friends,
day and night,
and now I am afraid to meet with my Beloved.
I must climb so many stairs
to reach my Beloved's palace;
my heart trembles.
And yet, I know, if I want to enjoy Love,
I must not be shy.
I must remove my veil, and expose my entire self.
My eyes must be like lamps, revealing my light.
Listen to me, my friend!
My Beloved understands the one who truly loves.
If you do not truly long for the Beloved One,
there's no point wearing jewelry,
and applying mascara and eye shadow
is just a waste of time.
Be naked.

GOD-IS-ME

There is a land
where doubt and sorrow have no power,
where the terror of death is no more.
There the forests are always blooming,
and the wind carries the fragrant scent of *God-is-me*.
There the bee of the heart draws deep
from the blossom of *God-and-I-are-one*
and desires no other joy.

ONLY LOVE

Beloved, not-created One,
who will serve You?
Each person who claims to follow You
is actually worshipping a god of their own creation.
So many people say they serve You,
and yet none of them truly seek You.
Everyone has their own ideas about You,
but You are always something different.
All the religious experts argue with each other—
but the person who knows the radiance of Your love
is the one who is made whole.

WORDS CAN NEVER CONTAIN CREATION

Where is the difference between
the ocean and its waves?
The ocean and its waves are one body.
When the wave rises, it is the water,
and when it falls, it is the same water again.
Can you see any difference?
Because we name the wave,
can it no longer be thought of as water?
Words can never contain Creation.
Within the Supreme Creator,
the worlds are strung like the beads of a rosary.
Look upon these prayer beads
with the eyes of wisdom.

SWING!

The minds swings
between the poles of the conscious
and the unconscious.
All beings and all worlds are swinging too,
and the swing never ceases its sway.
Swing!
Millions of beings are there in the swing:
the sun and the moon in their orbits are there.
Millions of ages pass, and the swing goes on.
Swing!
The sky and the earth and the air and the water,
all are swinging.
And God taking form in the world
swings!

THE MOMENTS
PERFORM THEIR ADORATION

Sunlight and moonlight and starlight
shed radiance like water.
Love's melody swells forth,
and the beat of love's detachment is its rhythm.
Day and night, the music fills the heavens.
My Beloved dazzles
like a lightning flash across the sky.
Even the moments perform their
adoration, each one in turn.
swaying its row of lamps;
day and night, the universe sings in worship.
Find the hidden banner and the secret canopy:
hear the sound of the unseen bells.
Here is the place where adoration never ends,
here the Lover of the Universe is enthroned.

THE COMMITTED SEEKER

The committed seeker merges within her
the double currents of love and detachment,
like the mingling of two rivers.
In her heart, the sacred Water flows day and night,
and the cycle of birth and death comes to an end.
See! Wonderful rest is found in the Spirit;
the one who readies herself for it, relaxes there.
Held by cords of love, the swing of the Ocean of Joy
sways to and fro,
and with a sound like thunder,
breaks into song.

THE MISPERCEPTIONS OF LIFE AND DEATH

See the lotus that blooms without water!
The bee of my heart drinks its nectar.
I am filled with awe,
gazing at the lotus that blooms at the heart
of the universe's spinning wheel.
Music flows from it, and my heart drinks
from the joy of the Infinite Sea.
Dive into that Ocean of sweetness!
Be washed clean
of all the misperceptions of life and death.
Here you will quench the thirst of your five senses,
and all misery will be no more.

THE RHYTHM OF LIFE AND DEATH

The Unlimited One is playing.
Look inside your heart
and see how the moonbeams of the Hidden One
shine within you.
Listen to the rhythm of life and death,
beating like a drum.
Delight swells, and all space is radiant with light.
The Unplayed Music fills everything,
the music of the Love that fills the three worlds.
A million suns and moons are burning like lamps,
the drum beats, and the Lover swings and plays.
Love songs ring out,
and light rains down in showers.
Taste the nectar of heaven.

Look at life and death, and see—
nothing separates them.
The right hand and the left hand
are one and the same.
Listen without speaking;
this truth cannot be found in any scripture or book.

SEEING WITHOUT SIGHT

I rest on the lap of the Self-Standing One.
I drink from the Cup of the Indescribable.
I hold in my hand the Key of the Mystery.
I have delved so deeply
I have reached the Root of Union.
Following the pathless way,
I have arrived in the Sorrowless Land.
Sweetly, easily, the kindness of my Beloved
falls on me.
They say God is infinite and unreachable,
but while meditating, I have seen without sight.

THE SORROWLESS LAND

This is the sorrowless land.
No one knows the path that leads here,
only the one who has risen above all sorrow.
This is the land of rest;
there is nothing you need do to earn it.
Here is the Ultimate Word—
but who can express its wonderful flavor?
The one who tastes it once
forever knows what joy it gives.
Knowing that, the ignorant become wise,
and the wise become speechless and silent.

TOTALLY DRUNK

I am totally drunk.
My ego is detached, no longer grasping.
I drink from the cup that overflows
with the in-breathings and out-breathings of love.
The whole sky rings out in sound,
with music made without fingers
and without strings.
If you merge your life with the Ocean of Life,
you will find your life in the Land of Delight.

SET FREE FROM FEAR

Every hour holds such busy joy.
I press time's grapes
and drink the essence of the hours.
I live in the life of the Creator.
I speak truth,
for now truth and I have grown together;
I have swept away all that is worthless,
and now I am set free from fear;
I see past the illusions of life and death.

ONLY NOW

The sky is filled with music; it rains nectar,
and the harp strings plink and tinkle,
while the drums beat.
What a secret splendor is there,
in the mansion of heaven!
There we no longer talk
about the rising and setting of the sun,
for in this sea of Divine manifestation—
which is the Light of Love—
day and night are no longer separated.
Time is united, and there is only *now*,
only joy, forever, without struggle,
joy that fills us to the brim,
as we see the Holy One playing.

THE PLAYFULNESS OF THE UNIVERSE

Now my body experiences
the playfulness of the universe,
for I have escaped the illusion of this world.
The inward and the outward have become one,
and the Infinite and the finite are united.
I am drunk with the sight of this All!
Your light, the Lamp of Love,
both fills the universe and fulfills it.
All illusion is gone,
and the conflict between life and death
has ended.

THE CELEBRATION OF THE BELOVED

Heaven's middle region, where our spirits dwell,
gleams with the music of Light.
There, where the pure, white music blossoms,
my Beloved plays, delighted.
Millions of suns and moons grow dim,
compared to the wondrous luminance
of a single Divine hair.
The rain, like nectar,
pours and pours, and never ceases.
Come, O Seeker of Truth!
See the celebration of the Beloved!

WAKE UP!

O my heart! The Spirit, the great One,
is near you: wake up!
Hear the Spirit, your Beloved,
who stands near your bed,
calling you.
You have slept for so long, age upon age.
Will you finally wake up?

THAT WHICH YOU ARE

Where do you think you are going, O my heart?
There is no road before you,
no fellow-traveler to follow.
See, nothing is moving here.
There is no water to cross,
no boat and no boatman.
There is not so much as a rope to tow the boat,
nor anyone to pull it.
No earth, no sky, no time, no thing.
There is neither body nor mind there.
Where can you quench the yearning of your soul,
when all you see is emptiness?
Be strong, and enter into your own body,
for you have a firm foothold there.

Stop seeking that which cannot
be grasped, O my heart.
Forget about all your ideas and illusions,
and stand fast in that which you are.

YOU WILL NEVER DIE AGAIN

Lamps burn in every house, O blind one!
And yet you cannot see them.
One day, your eyes will suddenly be opened,
and then you will see.
The fetters of death will fall from you,
and you will be free.
When that happens,
there is nothing you need to say or hear,
there is nothing you need to do.
You will be alive, yet dead,
and you will never die again.

YOUR BELOVED IS NEAR

The religious expert tells you
that God's home is far away.
But your Beloved is near;
you don't have to climb a tall tree to seek God.
Priests think they need to spend their lives
teaching people to have faith,
but the true fountain of life is within you.
Foolish one! God is right next to you—
and you have set up a stone to worship.
Religious practices, virtue, and vice—
these mean nothing to God.
You will never express how sweet is the Beloved
who lives within you.

THE TRUE TEACHER

My heart yearns for the true Teacher,
who fills the cup of true love,
drinks of it—and then offers it to me.
The Teacher removes the veil from our eyes,
so we can clearly see the Creator.
The Teacher reveals the worlds
that spin within God
and makes us hear the unplayed Music.
The Teacher shows us that joy and sorrow are one.
The Teacher fills all speech with love.
When we have a Teacher like this,
leading us to the shelter of safety,
we have no reason to fear.

LOSE YOURSELF

The evening shadows fall thick and deep,
and body and mind nestle in love's darkness.
Open your window to the west,
and lose yourself in the expanse of love.
Look in your heart and see the lotus there;
drink the nectar from its petals.
Leap into the sea,
and know that the waves will receive you.
Listen! Amid the sea's splendor,
the conches and the cockles are singing.
Look! The Beloved fills the vessel of my body.

A CREATURE OF TWO WORLDS

What do I cherish most?
When it comes down to it, it's this—
the Love that makes my life limitless,
even in this world,
for my life is like a lotus:
it lives in the water, and it blossoms in the water,
and yet the water never touches its petals,
for they open above the water, beyond its reach.
I too am a creature of two worlds,
living in this one,
yet blossoming in the other.

PARADOX

My Beloved hides from me,
and my Beloved leaps out before me.
My Beloved has set impenetrable
boundaries around my life;
and my Beloved has freed me from all limitation.
My Beloved brings me both sorrow and joy.
In the end, only my Beloved
can heal the gaps between these things.
I will give my body, my mind,
and my life to my Beloved,
and I will still be whole.

DRENCHED WITH GOD

The Sacred Sound created all things.
The primordial Sound of creation
is the shape of love,
yet formless, intangible, eternal.
Seek oneness with it!
The formless God takes a thousand forms,
yet remains infinite, fathomless, indestructible.
When God dances in rapture,
the world of form flows out
in waves from the dance.
Divine joy is too vast
for the human body or mind to contain.
All joy, all sorrow, all consciousness
is drenched with God,
the One who has no beginning or end,
the One who holds everything in joy.

THE UNKNOWN

The compassion of my Teacher
reveals the unknown to me.
My Teacher teaches me how to walk without feet,
how to see without eyes and hear without ears,
how to drink without using my mouth,
and fly without any wings.
Love and meditation bring me
into a land without light,
a place without sunlight or moonlight,
a world where there is no difference
between day and night.
I eat nothing there, and yet I taste
the sweetness of nectar;
I drink nothing, and yet my thirst is quenched.

The fullness of joy comes when we respond
with delight to the Unknown,
a joy that cannot be described with speech.
The Teacher is too vast to contain within words,
and I am blessed to be a disciple.

UNITY

The limited dances with the unlimited.
"You and I are one!"
they proclaim to the blast of a trumpet.
The Teacher comes in
and bows down before the disciple.
This is a wonder of wonders.

THE BIRD IN MY HEART

Within me is a tree
an on this tree, is a bird,
and the bird dances with the joy of life.
No one knows where this tree is;
no one knows where the birdsong comes from,
for the bird's nest is deep in the leaves' shadows.
The bird comes to its nest in the evening
and flies away when morning comes;
it never speaks a single word
of everything that it says.
No one ever told me
about this bird that sings within me;
no one ever needed to tell me.

The bird is neither colored nor colorless,
and it has no form.
It sits in the shadow of love.
It dwells with the Unreachable,
the Infinite, the Eternal,
and no one notices when it comes and goes.
Sister Seeker, Brother Pilgrim,
sink deep in this Mystery!
If you are wise, you will seek the place
where a bird is resting in your own heart.

DANCE!

Dance, my heart! Dance with joy!
The melodies of love
fill all the days and nights with music,
and the world listens.
Crazy with joy, life and death dance together,
swaying to the rhythm of the music.
The hills and the sea and the entire Earth dance.
The human world also joins the dance,
laughing and crying.
Why wear a monk's robe
and retreat from the world?
Look! My heart dances,
and I express my delight in a hundred creative arts,
giving joy to the Creator.

ONE

When you are drunk with love,
why would you need words?
I have wrapped the diamond in my cloak;
why should I open up my cloak again and again,
as though to prove what is there,
when I already know?
If both sides of the scale are full,
why bother with weighing?
When the swan has flown to the mountain lake,
why would she continue to search for food
in puddles and ditches?
Your Beloved dwells within you;
why do you need external proof?
Listen! My Beloved,
the One who ravishes me with loveliness,
is one with me.

UNBREAKABLE

How could the love between You and me break?
As the leaf of the lotus floats on the water,
so You are my Beloved,
and I am Your lover.
As the moon-eating partridge
gazes all night at the moon,
so You are my Beloved,
and I am Your lover.
From the beginning of time until time's end,
You and I have loved each other;
how could anything ever extinguish our love?
As the river enters the ocean,
so my heart flows into You.

THE LOVER'S ARROW

Wake up, my friend, and sleep no more!
The night is over and gone—
do you want to lose your day to sleep too?
Others who are already awake
are decked with jewels,
but you, foolish woman, have missed your chance.
You were asleep, and now your bed is empty,
for your Lover left you in the night.
But listen! Can you hear the music your Lover plays?
His music is like an arrow, piercing your heart.
Finally, you are awake.

THE ENDLESS BATTLE

Where does night go when the sun shines?
And if it is night, where has the sun gone?
The two can never be together.
And so where there is wisdom,
ignorance cannot endure,
but when ignorance is present, wisdom dies.
Where there is lust, there is no love,
but where there is love, there is no lust.
In the field of your body, a battle is raging.
The kingdom of truth, joy, and integrity
fights against hatred, selfishness, and greed.
In this battle, the strongest weapon
is the sword of God's Name.
When God enters the field,
all those selfish cowards run away.

But it is a long, hard fight,
this endless battle of the truth-seeker.
The war wages day and night,
for as long as life lasts.

LOVE'S KEY

If you get turned around,
the gate will lock behind you.
You can open it with love's key.
When you do, the Beloved will greet you.
Don't walk away!

THE SONG NEVER ENDS

Listen, my friend.
Your body is God's harp.
God tightens the strings
and plays love's melody.
When the strings snap
and the pedals grow slack,
the harp will return to dust,
for it was dust all along.
But the song was God's,
and the song never ends.

45

DON'T GO WANDERING

My home is where I meet God.
Within my home is life's joy;
why should I leave it and go traveling?
I can find either bondage or
freedom within my home,
depending on if I see God's truth.
The home is the place of your being,
the place where you learn to love,
without claiming anything as your own.
Your home gives you a ladder
to reach the One who is Real.
So don't go wandering. Stay where you are.
Be patient.
In time, all things will come to you there,
in your home.
You don't need to go looking for them.

OPEN EYES

Ever since I met my Beloved,
we have never stopped making love.
I don't shut my eyes when I pray,
I don't plug my ears,
I don't fast or practice any other discipline.
I simply look at the world
with my eyes open, smiling,
and I see Divine beauty everywhere.
Whatever I see, reminds me of God.
Whatever I do, becomes worship.
Day and night are the same for me;
all contradictions have become one.

DRENCHED WITH JOY

Wherever I go, I am moving through God.
Any work I do is service to God.
When I lie down at night,
I am prostrate in worship.
Because God is all things, God only do I love.
Now I never speak empty words—
I only sing God's glory.
Whatever I'm doing, I can never forget God,
for the rhythm of the Divine music
beats constantly within me.
My heart dances,
and I expose all that was once hidden within me,
for I am drenched in the joy
that rises above all pleasure and pain.

THE REAL IS YOUR HOME

Whenever I hear
about fish in the river who think they are thirsty,
I burst out laughing.
You're no different from those fish.
Don't you see that the Real is your home,
and you are already there?
But you wander here and there,
bored with your life,
always searching somewhere else for meaning.
Let me tell you something.
It doesn't matter if you travel to Paris
or Timbuctoo;
if you don't find your own soul,
everything you see will seem unreal.

CRAZY!

The sky is a banner,
bejeweled with the moon and the stars.
Look at the light!
Quiet your thoughts as you gaze at the splendor.
If you drink from this nectar,
you will dance and dance,
and everyone will think you are crazy.

FLEXIBLE

Who are You, Beloved?
Where do You come from?
Where do You live?
How is it that You play with creation?
The fire burns the wood,
but where was the fire before?
When the wood turns to ashes,
where did the fire go?
God is neither limited nor infinite
(but both).
God is happy to use whatever language
the listener will understand.

IT'S SIMPLE

Listen, seeker!
Practice self-discipline, but do it simply.
As the seed is within the tree,
and within the seed are flowers and fruit and shade,
in the same way,
the seed of Life is within your body,
and within that seed, you'll find your body again.
Apart from God, you cannot breathe air,
drink water, or warm yourself at a fire,
for God is in all things.
You breathe God, you drink God,
and God warms you.

WORD AND TRUTH

Listen, you who call yourself a scholar,
a person of great knowledge,
what is there that is not contained by the Soul?
If you put a pitcher of water on a lake,
the pitcher has water inside it and outside it.
Do not give this a name, don't create a term for it,
for if you do, you'll likely stumble
into the error of this or that,
one thing or another, but never both,
the fallacy whose name is
dualism.
Listen to the Word and the Truth,
which is the essence of who you truly are.
God speaks the Word.
God is the Creator.

THE GLORY OF FORMS

The tree of life
is a strange tree that has no roots
and bears fruit without ever blossoming.
It has no branches and no leaves;
it is nothing but light rising higher and higher.
Two birds sing in that tree;
one is the Teacher and the other the Disciple.
The Disciple keeps tasting the many fruit
that hang from the tree of life,
and meanwhile, the Teacher watches her with joy.
The tree and the birds can never be found,
and yet they are clearly visible everywhere.
The Formless is expressed by life's countless forms.
I sing the glory of forms!

THE UNLIMITED COLORS OF LOVE

My restless mind is quiet at last,
and my heart is luminescent,
for by looking closely at the This-ness of this world,
I have seen beyond This-ness.
In the company of my friends,
I have seen the One Friend.
Forever in bondage, I am forever free.
I have escaped the grip of all limitation.
My life cannot be contained
by anything that is narrow, constricted, or cramped.
I have reached what can never be reached,
and my heart wears the colors of love.

THE WAY OF LOVE
AND SURRENDER

That which you see is not Real,
and that which is Real cannot be expressed.
You say: "Unless I see, I won't believe,"
but the wise will hear what I'm saying.
Some seekers of God contemplate the Formless,
while others meditate on the form,
but those who are wise know God is beyond both.
Divine beauty cannot be seen with our eyes,
and the rhythm of the Divine music
cannot be heard with our ears.
But if you discover the way of love and surrender,
if you adore the world
while you put no claim on the world,
you will never die.

THE SONG OF LOVE

The Infinite never stops playing Her flute,
for it is the Song of love.
When love refuses to be limited,
it reaches truth.
The fragrance of the Song spreads
everywhere, infinitely,
for nothing can stand in its way.
The Song gleams like a million suns,
and it sings what nothing else can sing:
the melody of truth.

READY

I am ready to meet my Beloved.
As I grow older,
the pain of being separated from Him
makes my heart ache.
I wandered back and forth in the alleys of learning,
not knowing what I searched for,
but there in those alleys,
I received news of my Beloved.
I got a letter from Him
that contained a message I can never speak,
and now I am no longer afraid of death.
The Deathless One is now mine.

TRUE JOY

When I feel separate from my Beloved,
my heart hurts.
Nothing pleases me during the day,
and at night I cannot sleep.
But who can I talk to about these feelings?
Who would understand?
No one but my Beloved Herself.
The nights are so dark,
as I lie awake hour after hour.
Because I am not centered in my union with God,
I am anxious, fearful, even a little paranoid.
Listen, my friend!
Nothing will make you truly happy
until you have met your Beloved
and become one.

FINDING THE FOCUS

What is that flute music I hear?
What is this melody that thrills me with joy?
The flame burns without a lamp;
the lotus blossoms without a root;
but the moon-bird is devoted to the moon;
and with all its heart, the rain-bird longs for rain.
The Beloved longs for you, is devoted to you.
If you are His lover,
where should your life be focused?

THE SOURCE OF THE SONG

Can you hear the tune the Unsung Music is singing?
Listen, right there, where you are!
In whatever room you are,
you can hear the gentle song.
You don't need to go anywhere!
Trying to make yourself pure is also a waste of time.
If you haven't drunk from the nectar
of the One Love,
there's no point running here and there,
looking for the Source of the Song.

THE FOUNDATION
OF LOVE'S DELIGHT

The scholar searches the scriptures
and then teaches others,
but if his heart is not soaked with love,
what good does it do?
The religious person dyes her clothes scarlet,
but if she doesn't know the color of love,
the tint of her clothing means nothing.
Instead, wherever you are—
in a temple or in your house,
in the middle of the woods,
or in a flower garden—
wherever you are, know this:
God delights in you.

SHEER JOY

The path of love is not easy to see,
but once you are on it,
you no longer need to ask for anything;
you also no longer need
to stop yourself from asking.
There, you will lose yourself at the Beloved's feet.
There, you will plunge into the sheer joy of seeking;
you will be immersed in Love,
like a fish deep in the ocean.
You will leap up to serve your Beloved,
quick to demonstrate your love.
This has been my experience,
and now I share it with you.

THE FORM OF THE FORMLESS

The true spiritual teacher
can show you the form of the Formless
in ways your physical eyes can see.
She will teach you
that you need only simple things to reach God;
you do not need ceremonies and rituals.
She will not make you close all your doors,
hold your breath, and renounce the world.
Instead, she will show you how to sense the Spirit
in whatever thing your mind attaches itself to.

EVERYTHING I SEE IS GOD

The true teacher will teach you
to be still in the midst of your busyness.
You will enjoy all things,
while remaining immersed in Divine joy,
constantly one with God.
The infinite dwelling place of Infinite Being
is everywhere:
in earth, water, sky, and air.
With the strength of a lightning bolt,
a seeker is forever poised above the abyss.
The God who is within me
is the same God who is outside me.
Everything I see is God.

WITH YOUR WHOLE LIFE

Take for yourself the Word
that springs from the Universe!
That Word is the Teacher.
I have heard it and become a disciple.
But how many people know
the meaning of the Word?
O Seeker, practice saying the Word
with your whole life!
All the sacred writings proclaim it.
It is the foundation of the world.
Saints and wise ones talk about it.
But no one can fathom the mystery of the Word.

THE WORD

The houseowner leaves her house
when she hears the Word.
When the one who has given up on love
hears the Word,
he is reunited with love.
All philosophy interprets the Word,
and the practice of surrender points to it.
All world-forms grew from the Word.
The Word reveals all.
But who knows where the Word comes from?

MIND POISON

Drink up!

Get drunk!

Be intoxicated

with the sweetness of the Divine Name.

Listen, Seeker!

Apart from God,

your entire mind is filled with poison.

GOD IS LOVE

O human!
When you don't know your own Maker,
why are you so arrogant?
Forget about being smart.
All your words will never unite you with God.
Don't fool yourself,
thinking that because you know the scriptures,
you know God.
Love does not consist of any of these things,
but the person who seeks Love,
has already found God.

SUFFICIENCY

Wandering in the sea of eternal life,
I have everything I need;
I ask for nothing.
As the tree grows from the seed,
so does all spiritual disease emerge
from constant wanting.

DRINK!

When you reach the clear sea of joy,
do not go on your way thirsty.
Wake up!
Pure water is offered to you;
drink it in with your every breath.
Don't go searching after mirages,
wandering far from the only thing
that will truly quench your thirst.
The saints drank from this sea,
and now they are drunk with love;
they thirst only for love.

BE LIGHT!

Listen to me!
You no longer have to live within the box
that fear built.
But when you tell yourself lies,
you create your own prison.
You are carrying such a heavy load of desires;
how can you expect to float in the water of joy?
You are far too heavy.
Instead, be light.
Let it all go.
Keep only:
truth, detachment, and love.

EMPTY

Why are you so impatient, heart of mine?
The One who watches over birds,
beasts, and insects—
and all life—
the One who was already taking care of you
while you were in your mother's womb,
don't you think THAT One
will continue to care for you now?
O heart of mine,
why did you wander so far away from your Beloved?
How could you turn away
from your Beloved's smile?
You left your Beloved and relied on others instead.
Now, everything you do is empty.

SURRENDER EVERYTHING

How hard it is to meet my Beloved!
I must follow the example of the rain-bird,
who cries in thirst for the rain
but is willing to die
rather than accept any other water.
Or I must be like the deer
who is lured by the music;
she knows she will be killed as she listens,
and yet she is not afraid.
I hear the voice of the rain-bird and the deer,
and I shout into my own ear:
"Stop being so worried about your poor old body!
Surrender everything,
and then you will no longer fear death."

I NO LONGER CARED

When I had lost the Way,
my true Teacher showed it to me again.
So I stopped participating in rites and ceremonies;
I no longer washed myself with holy water.
People said I was crazy,
while they claimed to be sane.
They said my craziness bothered them.
But I no longer cared.
Now I will not ring the temple bell.
I will not worship before statues that are mere idols.
I will not place flowers before dead images.
Fasting and disciplining the body with pain,
those things are not what pleases God.

THE TRUE NAME

If you stripped yourself of everything you love
and refused to use your five senses,
God would not be happy.
Here is what DOES please God:
the person who is kind and practices generosity,
who doesn't takes sides in the world's controversies,
who loves all Earth's creatures
as much as she loves herself.
That is the person who will enter
the never-dying Being,
and the true God will always be with her.
So speak with integrity;
surrender your pride;
and you will learn the true Name
of the One who never dies.

BOUND

Look at that guy who thinks he's so smart!
He has dyed his clothes—
but he hasn't soaked his mind in the colors of love.
He has pierced his ears,
grown his beard down to his belly,
let his hair turn into matted locks,
and now he looks like a goat.
He went out into the wilderness
to castrate his physical desires,
and now he is a eunuch.
He reads the scriptures
and never stops talking about them.
He sits in the temple,
but instead of worshipping the true God,
he worships a stone.

Here is what I have to say:
that poor guy has bound himself hand and foot
to death.

YOUR OWN HEART

What is my God like, I wonder.
The preachers shout their opinions:
Is their God deaf?
My God's ears are so sharp,
She hears the tiny tinkle
of the anklet on an insect's leg.
If you make a show of your religion,
letting everyone know how holy you are,
your own heart will be a threat to your self-image.
When that's the case,
how can you be united with the true God?

THE RHYTHM OF THE WORLD

When I hear the melody of my Beloved's flute,
I expand beyond my boundaries.
The flower opens its petals
(even though it is not spring),
and the bee is already invited to drink from it.
The heavens roar like a lion,
lightning streaks across the sky,
and waves thunder in my heart.
As the rain descends, I yearn for my Beloved.
The rhythm of the world rises and falls,
drawing my heart with it.
I see the hidden banners unfurled across the sky,
fluttering in the wind.
My heart surrenders to death—
and yet lives.

GOD'S DANCE

If God is contained within a building,
then to whom does the entire world belong?
If you limit your image of God to a single thing,
you won't know what you have left out.
Allah, Brahma, Jesus, Buddha:
these are all names that ultimately point
to the same One.
If you could see inside your heart,
you'd see them all there,
dancing with their hands joined.
Besides, each woman and man who has ever lived
is God's living form.
I too am a child of God,
and God alone is my Teacher and Guide.

WHOSE SHAPE IS LOVE

The person who is humble, contented,
who has balanced perceptions,
whose thoughts are occupied
with mature acceptance and rest,
she is the one who has seen God
and touched God.
All fear and despair have departed from her.
The constant thought of God is like sweet lotion;
everything delights her.
Both her work and her rest hum
with the melody of God;
love radiates from her.
Reach up and touch God,
the One, indivisible, unchangeable, peaceful,
the One who fills every container
to its brim with joy,
the One whose shape is love.

FOCUS

Make goodness your companion;
live in the dwelling place of the Beloved One.
Take all your thoughts and direction from there.
How can you host a wedding reception,
if the Bridegroom is missing?
Stop wavering; focus your thoughts on the Beloved.
Don't attach yourself to other gods;
when you worship anything else but God,
your heart conveys no worth to you.
You will never find the Beloved that way!

THE JEWEL

We dropped the jewel in the mud,
and now we are all looking for it.
Some search in the east, some in the west,
some among the stones.
But I have found the jewel.
I see its true value,
and so I have carefully wrapped it
within the robe of my heart.

THE END AND THE BEGINNING

When the limousine came
to take me to my Lover's home,
my heart shivered with joy;
but the driver dropped me off
in the middle of a forest,
where I had no one and nothing to call my own.
O driver, I beg you, wait! Don't leave me here alone!
Take me back to my family and friends.
At least give me a chance to say goodbye.
Let me settle my affairs.
But voices sing in the air,
"O Seeker! Your business no longer matters.
You are done with buying and selling.
You are going to a new land now,
one where there are no malls or shops.

You are done with all that you consider bad
and also all that you consider good.
This is the end of everything.
And this is the beginning of everything."

THE PAIN OF YOUR OWN CHOICES

O heart of mine!
You do not know the hidden
ways of the city of love.
You came here in ignorance;
do you want to also return in ignorance?
What have you done
with this life you've been given?
You are carrying around in your head
a load of stones;
will you let someone take a few of them?
Look! Your Friend is standing right there,
just on the other side of the water,
but you never consider how you
might cross the water.
Your boat is broken.

You sit here at the edge of the water,
while the waves crash over you,
and you never move.
Who will be your friend
when you reach the end of your life?
You have never sought your heart's Companion,
and now you feel the pain of your own choices.

LIGHT

The scriptures say that the One above all variations
stands beyond this world
with its changing conditions.
Woman, why argue about whether
Divinity is beyond all
—or in all?
If you see everywhere as your home,
no pleasure or pain will fog your perception.
In that place of constant belonging,
Ultimate Reality is continuously revealed.
Light is Divinity's garment,
and the same light on which God sits
rests also on your head.
True God
is all Light.

THE SECRET OF LOVE

Open your eyes.
Look from the perspective of love
and see the One who saturates this world.
This is your own land, the place where you belong.
When you meet the true Teacher,
She will wake you up.
She will tell you the secret of love;
you will learn that love and detachment
are the same,
and then you will know
without question or doubt
the One who flows into this universe.

THE DIVINE JOKE

This world is the place where
you may discover Truth,
but you so easily become lost,
enchanted by the maze of paths.
Look! You don't have to go anywhere
to reach your goal!
You don't even need to cross the road.
This is the joke that never ends,
where myriad joys dance constantly
around the Beloved.
This title of this joke is "Eternal Bliss,"
where all getting is over,
and all giving up is done as well.
Here, the fire of possession
will never sear you again.

ALIVE WITH JOY

The Beloved's name is Ultimate Rest,
rest without limit,
and He has spread His love everywhere.
Truth is like a ray of Light
from which new things constantly spring forth,
and the Beloved is in all these things.
Look! Gardens and forests, thickets and clearings,
all are in blossom,
and the air is alive with joy.
Watch while the swan plays her wonderful game.
Listen while the Unplayed Music
ripples like water around the Infinite One.
The Beloved cannot be grasped.
He is Being itself.
A single one of his hairs
shines brighter than a million suns.

THE HARP OF LIFE

The road you follow through life is like a harp,
where your passage makes melodies
that pierce the heart.
Listen! The Eternal Spring is bubbling,
creating the endless stream of birth and death
that is life.

THE NAMELESS ONE

They call the Beloved
Emptiness,
She who is the Truth of truths,
in whom all truths are stowed.
Within Her Being, creation never ends.
This is beyond all philosophy,
for philosophy can never reach
far enough to grasp Her.
O my friend! See the Nameless One,
the One whom no words can describe.
You will only know Her
when you have reached Her country.
Then you will realize
that She is nothing like anything
that has ever been said about Her.

NO WORDS

In the final homeland there is no shape,
no body, no length, and no width;
how can I describe it to you?
When you reach the Way of the Endless One,
Divine grace will fall around you,
and then you will be set free
from all birth and all death.
I cannot put this into words,
neither with my mouth nor on paper.
If I try, I am like a person
seeking to describe the taste of honey,
though I have no voice.
The experience is real,
but there are no words to contain it.

A MILLION SUNS

O Self! Let us go to the land
where my Beloved lives.
In that land, Love fills her pitcher from the well,
though She has no rope
by which to pull the water up.
The sky is always clear there,
and yet the rain streams like liquid light.
O bodiless one within me!
Get up off your doorstep!
Get out there, where you can be soaked in the rain.
Dance in the moonlight,
for no night is ever dark there,
nor is one sun enough to illumine this vast land.
See! The rays that shine around you
are from a million suns.

NO LONGER AFRAID

Seeker of wisdom, hear what I have to say to you!
My words have no time stamp;
they will never expire.
If you want what is good for you,
you will listen closely and ponder what I have to say.
You have separated yourself from your Creator,
the One from whom you sprung;
you have lost your common sense,
for you have been seeking death instead of life.
All ideas, all doctrines, all wisdom
spring from the Beloved.
They grow from Him.
Once you realize the certainty of this,
you will no longer be afraid.

GOOD NEWS

Listen! I have good news to share with you!
Whose name have you been singing?
On whom have you been meditating?
Free yourself from the lies you've been told.
Why seek shelter in the emptiness of a vacuum?
If you set your Teacher at a distance
from your own heart,
then it is the distance you are honoring,
rather than your Teacher.
If it's true that God is so far away,
then who is creating the world,
the reality that's all around you at this minute?
When you make the mistake
of thinking God is not here,
you wander further and further,
constantly yearning for that
which you can never find.

PERMEATED WITH GOD

When you have put God so far away from you,
it's no wonder you can't reach Her!
When you realize how near She is,
then you will know the reality of Her joy.
"I don't want you to hurt anymore," she says to you,
"and that is why I have permeated
your being with My own.
Get to know yourself, for I am in every bit of you,
from your toes to your hair.
Make yourself stable and steady within yourself;
then you will sing,
and you and I will both be glad."

THE UNCONDITIONED AND THE CONDITIONED

The true Name is like no other name!
The only difference between the Conditioned
and the Unconditioned
is a tiny prefix two letters long.
The Unconditioned is the seed
from which blossoms the flower and then the fruit.
The Unconditioned is the Essence
of all other essences,
the Ground of all ground.
The Name is the root of all knowledge.
Find the Root, and true happiness shall be yours.
The Root will take you to the branch, the leaf,
the flower, and the fruit:
This is how you encounter God.

When the Unconditioned and the Conditioned
are no longer separated,
you will have found your heart's delight.

ONLY GOD

In the beginning, was only God:
formless, colorless Being,
Being with no descriptors, no conditions.
There was no beginning, no middle, no end,
for there was no time.
Then were no eyes, no darkness, no light,
no ground, no air, no sky, no fire,
no water, no earth, no rivers, no seas,
no oceans, and no waves.
There was neither sin nor righteousness;
there were no scriptures.
Even now, as in the beginning, the Supreme Being
cannot be confined to a single name.

The Life-Giver cannot be pinned down,
not by words, not by places, not by time;
formless but not vague,
without quality but always distinct,
the Beloved fills all.

THE DIVINE GAME

Reality is a game of joy,
brought into being by the Creator.
When God said, "Yes!"
all Creation sprang into being.
The Earth is God's delight,
and the sky fills God with joy.
The sun's blaze and the moon's glimmer
thrill the Creator.
The beginning, the middle, and the end:
they all make God happy.
The Beloved's joy is found everywhere:
in eyes and darkness, nerves and light;
in the Atlantic and the Pacific;
the Amazon, the Nile, the Ganges,
and the Mississippi;
the Sahara and the Mohave;
the Alps and the Himalayans and the Rockies.

Your Teacher is One,
and life and death, union and separation,
are all ways in which the Teacher plays in joy.
God plays in earth and water, soil and sky.
The whole universe is the Divine Game.
In play, God unfurls all Creation
and holds it steady.
You and me, the entire world,
all rest in the Divine Game
that is constantly being played,
and yet still we do not know
the One who is playing.

MEETING THE BELOVED

Music ripples from the harp strings,
and without hands or feet, the dance continues.
This is music that's played without fingers
and heard without ears,
for God is the Ear, and God is the Listener.
The garden gate is locked,
but the scent of the garden cannot be captured.
Inside, you will meet the Beloved.
but no one will see your encounter,
and only the wise will understand.

NO MATTER WHAT

The Beggar is begging,
but I cannot catch a glimpse of Her.
What shall I ask of the Divine Beggar,
when She gives me everything I need
without me ever asking?
I belong to Her,
and so I say, "Let events happen as they will!
No matter what, I am Hers!"

THE ENDLESS PATH
TO A MILLION GATES

I cry out loud for my Lover.
Unless I can be with Him in His home, I am lost.
It doesn't matter if I'm wandering
on an endless journey
or living in a mansion;
without my Beloved, nothing satisfies me,
and my mind and my body are both uneasy.
I know my Lover's home has a million gates,
and yet a vast sea separates it from me.
How can I get across?
I can see a path, but it stretches out forever,
never reaching the horizon.
My heart is a harp.
When its strings break, it becomes useless,
but if its strings are strung correctly,
then its music carries me to Love's home.

103

MORNING JOY

Laughing, I say to my parents,
"I must leave you in the morning,
for I am going to my Beloved."
"Don't go!" they say, angry with me,
and then they turn to each other
and shake their heads.
"She thinks she can make her Beloved
give her whatever she wishes,
but it's only her ego talking.
That's why she's so impatient to leave us."
Ah, but they don't know the truth!
I lift my veil, for now I am ready
to meet my Beloved.
This is the night for love.
My heart pounds with eagerness.
Imagine the joy that will be mine
in the morning!

WAKE UP!

Serve the One
who has entered the temple of your life!
Don't be shallow or foolish,
for the night is passing fast.
God has been waiting for you for countless ages;
because God loves you so much,
She has given you Her heart.
And all the while, you never knew
how close She was,
for you were sleeping.
Listen! That bell you hear is chiming for you.
"Wake up!" it says. "Your time of joy has come.
Your Beloved is waiting to caress you,
and Her love will have no end."

RAIN

The clouds are growing thick.
Do you hear the rumble of their voices?
Look there, to the east!
See the curtain of rain that is coming?
Are your fences in good shape?
Have you marked your boundaries?
Be careful the rain does not wash away your fields.
Instead, plow the soil, preparing it for salvation.
Let the seedlings of love
and the saplings of surrender
soak up the moisture
Be wise.
Because of this storm, the harvest comes.
Fill all your baskets,
so you can feed everyone you meet.

THE DIVINE GUEST

This is the best day of my life,
for today my Beloved is my guest.
I am making my bedroom and my garden beautiful,
preparing them for His Presence,
and while I work, I sing His name with longing.
Now He has arrived!
I wash His feet; I look into His face;
and I offer Him my body, my mind,
and all that I have.
O happiest of days!
My Beloved, my Treasure,
is here with me in my house!
All that is broken and sore has been healed,
as I touch Him with my love.

THIS IS GOD!

Are there people who are wise enough to hear
the unfathomable music that falls from the sky?
For God, the Source of all music,
makes all who are empty
FULL.
And God rests there in that fullness.
If you are centered in your body, however,
you will never be satisfied,
for you are seeking something that is incomplete.
Listen! From the sky falls the song,
deeper and louder:
God is this! This is God!
Love and surrender have become one.
This is the Beginning, this is the Word
that exists at the foundation of all else.

NOT IN ABSTRACTIONS

Who can teach you about God?
Remember, you will never find the forest,
if you are ignoring the tree.
The Beloved can never be found
in abstractions and generalizations.
God is always specific.

A LOAD OF ROCKS

I am very good with words.
Are you impressed?
But what good does my skill do me,
if I am floating without an anchor,
thirsting to death and burning up with desire?
"Hey you!" calls the Beloved.
"Why are you carrying that load
of rocks on your head?
Let your pride and your vanity drop into the dust.
And then, free and light,
come out and meet Me here!
Be Mine."

WAITING FOR LOVE

To comfort herself, the lonely woman keeps busy,
turning her spinning wheel
while she yearns for her Lover.
The body rises up like an entire city,
and within it, you have built
the palace that is your mind.
See, the wheel of love, spinning in the sky?
Rest yourself here, on the jeweled seat of wisdom,
where you can reach to spin the wheel.
See how delicately and meticulously
the woman makes her thread?
With love and reverence,
she spins it fine and strong,
and then she uses it to thread her loom.
"Look," she says. "I am weaving a banner
that unites all my days and nights,
while I wait for my Lover's touch."

COMPLETION

Millions of suns and moons and stars
shine beneath the great canopy of my Beloved.
God is the Mind within my mind,
the Eye within my eye.
If only I could make my eyes see
as far as my mind does!
If my love could only reach out and touch my Lover!
For love and the Lover must be united.
Only then will I be complete.

HOME-GOING

When I was young,
I came with my Beloved to His home,
but I did not live with Him,
nor did I taste Him,
and my younger years flew by like a dream.
On my wedding night,
my women friends sang together,
anointing me with the scented lotions
of both pleasure and pain,
but once the ceremony was finished,
I left my Lover and ran away.
I found another lover,
who consoled me on my long journey,
and now, together, we shall return
to the Divine Home.

Then, when we are there
in the Presence of the Beloved,
I shall blow on my trumpet
a great blast of joy and triumph,
for I shall be home at last.

HOW LOVE WORKS

O my soul, my inner self, my dear friend,
think carefully!
If you are really in love,
why are you still sleeping?
If you have found your Beloved,
then give yourself away completely,
and in return, take your Beloved for your own.
Why do you misplace your Beloved again and again?
If your eyes are already half shut with sleep.
why waste your time making the bed
and arranging the pillows?
This is how love works:
you surrender everything inside your head,
and then you burst out laughing.

SEEK GOD WITHIN YOU

God is in me, and God is in you,
just as Life is in every seed.
Put away all your arrogance.
Shed your ego, the false self,
and seek God within you.

THE CENTER OF THE WORLD

A million suns are blazing with light,
and blue spreads like an ocean across the sky.
I sit here, at the center of the world,
and the fire of my desire cools,
as all the stains on my mind are washed clean.
Listen! Do you hear the ringing
of the bell that has no clapper?
Do you hear the beat of the drums
that are never struck?
Delight yourself in love!
Dance in the rain that pours down from the sky,
and never get wet.
The rivers stream with light,
and the entire world is steeped in Divine Love,
but only a few people experience it fully.

ALL I NEED

Many folks try to use the light of reason to see God,
but they remain blind,
for reason is actually the cause of their blindness.
The House of Reason is built far
from the House of God.
I am so blessed, for I have my own vessel
to fill with Divine joy.
The song I sing erases sorrow.
No matter how many times things come and go,
no matter how many goodbyes and hellos I say,
the melody remains unbroken.
Who needs reason?
All I need is love.

THE SPRING OF THE YEAR

As the season of spring blossoms,
I yearn to be united with my Lover.
How shall I find words for my Beloved's beauty?
All beauty merges together within Her.
Her colors are in every piece of art every created;
they cast a spell over both my body and my mind.
This is the game spring plays with God,
a game with no words,
whose only rule is beauty.

LISTEN!
SEE!

Pause the back-and-forth swing you call love.
Hang the dangling chains of the body and the mind
between the arms of the Beloved,
and relax into the ecstasy of love's joy.
Let tears stream like rain from your eyes,
and cover your heart with the blanket of the night.
Put your lips against your Beloved's ear,
and speak of the deepest desires of your heart.
Listen! See!
Focus on the vision of your Beloved.
Hear only the song He sings.

Love Prayers
from Rumi & Other Sufi Mystics

Pray with the Sufis!

The Sufi mystics' experience of God was down-to-earth, sometimes even crude, and always both practical and jubilant. Their religion was love—and God was their Beloved. Their relationship with the Beloved gave each moment meaning and joy.

As you pray with words inspired by Rumi and other Sufi mystics, you'll experience a new understanding of the Divine One who is everything and nothing, all that we can perceive and all that we cannot. You may even, like the Sufis, find yourself falling head over heels in love with a God who is present everywhere, within you and without. Whatever your religion (or lack of religion), these spiritual poems, inspired by ancient Sufism, will bring you into a deeper relationship with both the Divine and your true Self.

Song of a Christian Sufi
A Spiritual Memoir

This is the story of a woman's spiritual journey: from the restrictions of growing up as Catholic female in the 1950s to her emotional and spiritual liberation as a Sufi—and to her ultimate return to a new understanding of Christianity. Building on the foundations of the Sufi and Christian mystics, Della Penna's memoir is sometimes funny, sometime heartbreaking—and always points toward more universal truths beyond the particularities of an individual life. It will resonate with anyone seeking to find life's deeper meanings. The author's discovery of her own unique "song" is truly a gift to us all!

Brother Lawrence
A Christian Zen Master

Brother Lawrence's spiritual journey made him stand out to the Christian community of his day (he lived c. 1614-1691), not because he was a great thinker, a gifted speaker, or a talented writer—but simply because of the way he lived his life. This way of life echoes the teachings of Zen. Surrender yourself to God and you will be equally at peace in both suffering and joy.

Jesus and Lao Tzu
Adventures with the Tao Te Ching

"How can I describe this book? If I say it is brilliant, crazy, hilarious, sobering, vulgar, and sublime, all those words are true—but they are certainly not enough to express the contents of *Jesus and Lao Tzu*. The book defies being categorized or neatly summarized. It will have to suffice if I say simply this: the book's words make me happier, freer, and wiser. If you read it with an open heart, I predict it will do the same for you."

— Kenneth McIntosh, author of *Water from an Ancient Well: Celtic Spirituality for Modern Life.*

The Heart of Meditation
Thoughts, Prayers, & Meditations

In this collection, author George Breed offers bite-size entries into mindfulness and transformation. Each meditation could be used as a vehicle for greater consciousness—or as a prayer leading to deeper awareness of spiritual reality and being.

One Amazon reviewer summarized: "Each tiny gem of a meditation holds meaning beyond and beneath the words, and each provides nourishment for the mind and the heart. Concise, simple, but packed with a powerful load of thought-provoking enlightenment, George Breed gives more to us in his meditations with a dozen or so words than most philosophers give in twelve dozen."

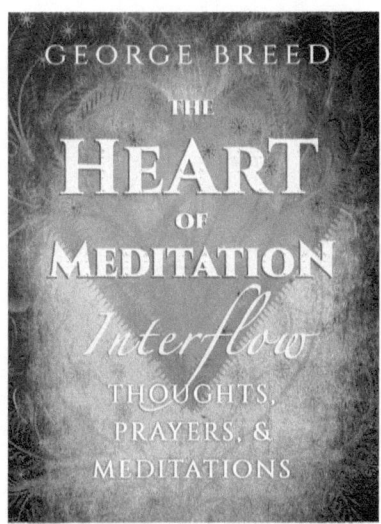

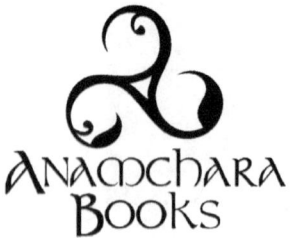

AnamcharaBooks.com

www.ingramcontent.com/pod-product-compliance
Lightning Source LLC
Chambersburg PA
CBHW020442090526
44586CB00045B/667